This book was written with good intentions.

This book belongs to

_____

ISBN: 978-1-990336-99-7

2nd Edition

Contact the publisher for Library and Archives Canada catalogue information.

ALANNA RUSNAK PUBLISHING
Alanna Rusnak Publishing is an imprint of Chicken House Press
chickenhousepress.ca

FOR ALL FAMILIES

OPENNESS
COMPASSION
UNITY

mommy & me

a story about mental health

Mommy and me do things together

because I love my mommy
and my mommy loves me.

Mommy and me go skating and sliding.

I love my mommy and
my mommy loves me.

Mommy and me bake cookies and cupcakes.

I love my mommy and my mommy loves me.

Mommy and me play games and watch movies.

I love my mommy and my mommy loves me.

Sometimes my mommy doesn't feel good.

Sometimes my mommy's brain doesn't feel good,

and mommy says mean things...

not because I'm bad.

Does that make me sad?

Or does that make me mad?

Mommy and me talk later about our feelings...

when we feel better, we do things together...

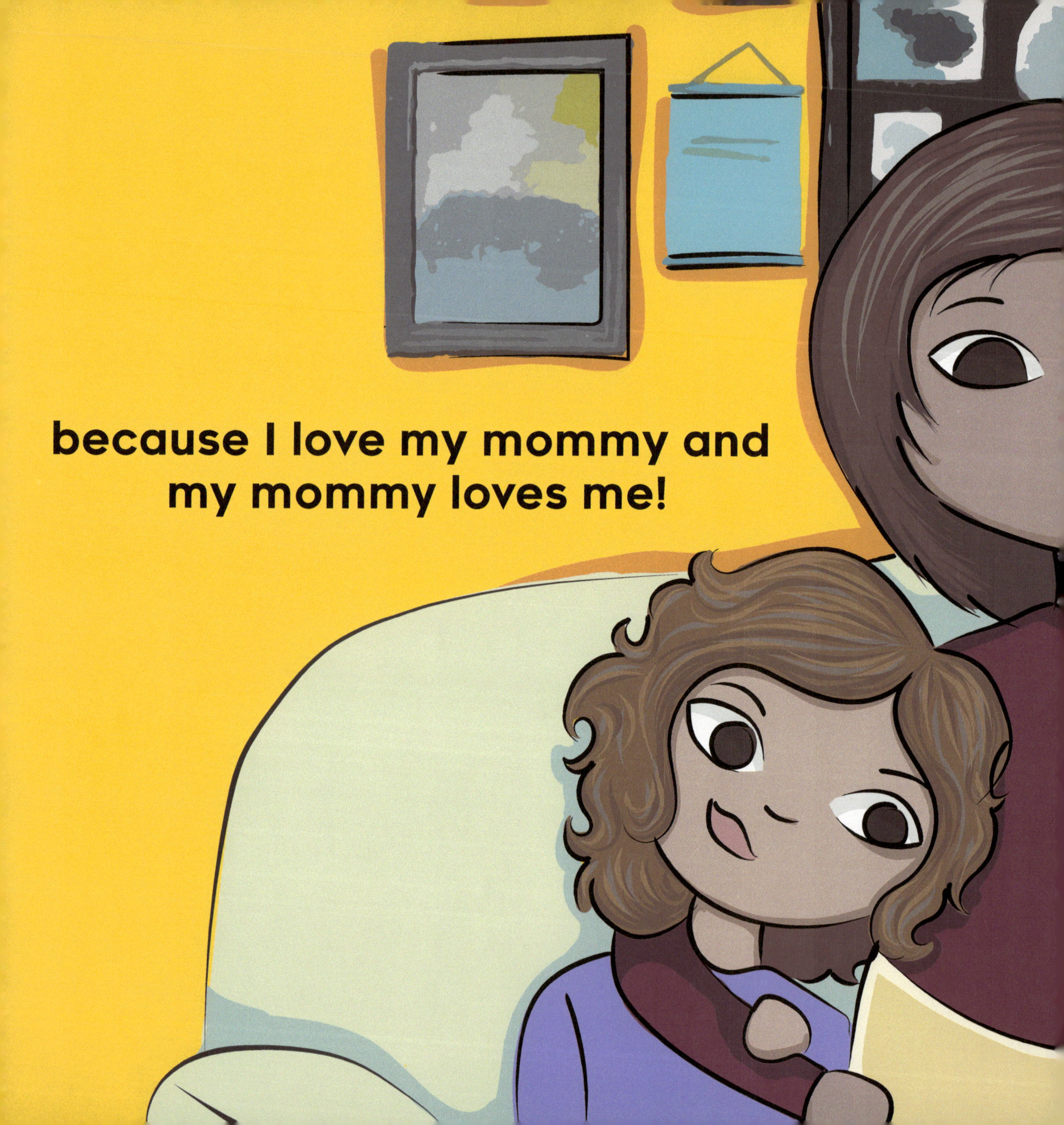

because I love my mommy and my mommy loves me!

THE BEGINNING

Remember to be kind.

A Note to Parents/Caregivers:

Mental health conditions affect people from all walks of life. In families, when adults struggle with their mental well-being, children notice changes, but often lack the words or understanding to process what they are seeing and feeling. This book was born from my desire to provide a gentle resource that could help bridge that gap.

For many years, I have been advocating for mental health awareness and understanding. My career as an educator brought me to the realization that families face various challenges showing me how important open conversation can be, especially with children.

I believe that awareness and understanding can begin at a very young age. Sometimes, it must begin early because families are already living with these realities. My hope is that it promotes empathy, acceptance, and most importantly, conversation.

Discovering my ancestral roots has added another important dimension to this work. Through gaining Cultural Knowledge about the Medicine Wheel, I've come to appreciate more deeply how finding balance as individuals contributes to balance in our families and communities. Healing—both personal and collective—is essential for our overall well-being. Sharing this story may help us on our journey.

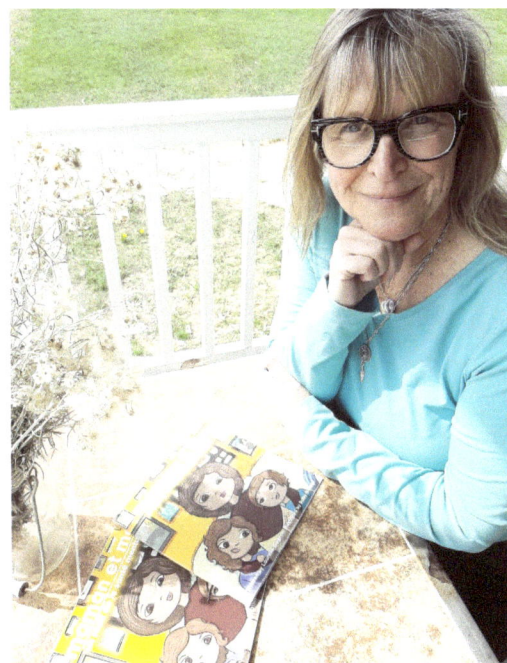

The children are our future generations who will help shape a world of love, unity, equality, forgiveness, peace, harmony, and joy. When you read this book with a child, you open a door to communication about mental health that may also change how we, as adults, communicate with each other.

My goal remains simple: to keep families talking and working together, for the good of all.

Laurelle

Personal notes
(You can write and draw in this book!)

www.ingramcontent.com/pod-product-compliance
Lightning Source LLC
LaVergne TN
LVHW072133070426
835513LV00002B/92